WRECKAGE

WRECKAGE

SALLY STUBBS

Wreckage
first published 2009 by
Scirocco Drama
An imprint of J. Gordon Shillingford Publishing Inc.
© 2009 Sally Stubbs

Scirocco Drama Editor: Glenda MacFarlane
Cover design by Terry Gallagher/Doowah Design Inc.
Author photo by Mits Naga Photography
Printed and bound in Canada on 100% post-consumer recycled paper.

We acknowledge the financial support of the Manitoba Arts Council, The Canada
Council for the Arts and the Government of Canada through the Book Publishing
Industry Development Program (BPIDP) for our publishing program.

Library and Archives Canada Cataloguing in Publication

Stubbs, Sally, 1954-
　　Wreckage / Sally Stubbs.

A play.
ISBN 978-1-897289-42-6

　　I. Title.

PS8637.T86W74 2009　　C812'.6　　C2009-904297-5

J. Gordon Shillingford Publishing
P.O. Box 86, RPO Corydon Avenue, Winnipeg, MB Canada R3M 3S3

For Mom

Acknowledgements

The author wishes to thank the many people—colleagues, friends, and family—who have inspired, supported, an belived in *Wreckage*. Special thanks to: Hrant Alianak, Martin Kinch and the Playwrights Theatre Centre, Brian Parkinson, Sally Clark, Chris Cinnamon, Joan Bryans, Susan Bonham, Elizabeth Dancoes, Stephen Drover, Del Surjik, Fran Gebhard, the talented casts and creative teams involved in workshop and full productions of the play, and Gordon Shillingford and Glenda MacFarlane. Finally, deepest gratitude and love to Mits, Mom, and Rod.

Sally Stubbs

Sally Stubbs is an award-winning playwright, teacher-director, and a performer who loves to clown. Most recently she was honoured to have received the third annual Canadian Peace Play Competition Award (2009) for her script *Herr Beckmann's People*, and the Gordon Armstrong Playwrights' Rent Award (2008). She is currently completing a graduate degree in writing at the University of Victoria with master playwright Joan MacLeod.

Sally's plays scheduled for production in the 2009-2010 season are her most recent recent script, *Herr Beckmann's People*, and *Wreckage*. A short independent film, *Mother Cutter*, was adapted from a section of *Wreckage*: the film was honoured as one of the "Best of Alberta Shorts" at the Calgary International Film Festival.

Sally's scripts include *Faroland*, *Centurions (in process)*, *Eyes. Two*, *She'll to the Wars*, *Home Movies*, *and Spinning You Home*, which she is currently adapting as a novel for young adults. Sally is a member of the Playwrights Guild of Canada.

Characters

Wreckage must be played by no fewer than six actors and, ideally, the cast will consist of seven performers. One actor plays Violet/Rose, another performs the roles of Virgin Mary and Mother Cutter as well as ensemble. A seventh actor would play Druggie and ensemble. Note: It is also possible to stage the play with two actors playing the characters of Violet and Rose.

Violet:
: A gorgeous young woman, twenty-five years old. She gets her looks from her mother, Rose, who she searches for in 1949.

Rose Wood:
: Real name is Lucy Plant. Early to mid-twenties. She has been missing since the crash of the Red Dragon in 1924.

Frank Cardinal:
: An employee of the Canadian Pacific Railway Police. An orphan, he was raised with Rose. In 1949 scenes he is an opium addict and walks with a limp due to a gunshot wound.

Momma:
: Real name is Anna Bigellini. A powerful, sexy gangster in the 1920s. Violet's Grand Momma.

Big Man:
: Real name is Shannon Bigellini. Momma's son, Rose's husband, Violet's Poppa.

Johnny:
: Works for Momma. He's her 'muscle' and younger lover.

Virgin Mary:
: Church statue comes to life.

Mother Cutter:
: Skid Row hag who performs abortions.

Druggie:
: Colourful Skid Row addict.

Ensemble:
: 'Rose' on initial train wreck as envisioned and 'written' by Violet; members of Momma's gang; passengers waiting in Kamloops train station; voice of the conductor.

Production Credits

Wreckage premiered at New West Theatre, under the Artistic Directorship of Brian Parkinson, in Lethbridge, AB, on October 13, 2005, with the following cast:

ROSE/VIOLET .... Kathy Zaborsky
MOMMA .... Sheila Mason
BIG MAN .... Jordon Navratil
FRANK CARDINAL .... Fred Hillyer
JOHNNY .... David Barruss

Directed by Gail Hanrahan
Set Design by David Barrrus
Lighting Design by Bob Stanford
Sound Design by Stacy Green
Costume Design by Leslie Robison-Greene
Stage Manager: Sara Turner

The Tightrope Productions' production of *Wreckage* premiered at Playwrights Theatre Centre, Vancouver, on May 16, 2007, with the following cast:

ROSE/VIOLET .... Tosha Doiron
MOMMA .... Joan Bryans
BIG MAN .... Adam Lolacher
FRANK CARDINAL .... James Behenna
JOHNNY .... Seth Ranaweera
VIRGIN MARY .... Kristina Murphy
MOTHER CUTTER/DRUGGIE .... Frances Herzer

Directed by Sally Stubbs
Set Design by Nicole Boyd
Lighting Design by Darren W. Hales
Sound and riginal Music by Catalin Ursu
Costume Design by Stephanie Koropatnick
Stage Manager: Vera Ha

Setting

The play takes place in the 'shadow' of the wreckage of The Red Dragon, a private railway coach. Action occurs in 1923, 1924, and 1949 on a train and in various locations in Kamloops and Vancouver, British Columbia. The wreck should overshadow the world of the play. Perhaps locations actually 'grow ' out of the wreck. Light, shadow, sound and smoke will be important elements in defining this Noir Canadiana setting.

Development History

Wreckage won an Honourable Mention in the 2005 Herman Voaden Playwriting Competition (Jurors' 'Top 5'), Queen's University.

The play was workshopped and received a public reading as part of the National Arts Centre (Ottawa) English Theatre 'On the Verge' New Play Reading Festival 2004; was selected for the 2004 Canadian Plays in Development Program, the University of Lethbridge; received a workshop production in the 2003 New Play Festival, Playwrights Theatre Centre, Vancouver; and received dramaturgical support from Hrant Alianak, Alianak Theatre Productions, Toronto.

Production Notes

All actors in central roles, except the one playing Big Man, must play their characters in at least two different times in their lives: the 1920s and 1949. In addition, the actor playing both Violet and Rose will need to transform onstage to create two distinct characters. The challenge for the actors will, of course, be to effect these transformations quickly, subtly, and obviously.

Due to the many shifts between time and place in the play, transitions are suggested in the script to allow for actors, and particularly Rose/Violet, to move and transform. This is a complex play and it is essential to focus on clarity, simplicity, some kind of consistency and, I believe, theatricality in these transitions.

As for playing style, I believe it is worth stressing that the stories of the past spring from three 'colourful' sources: the diary of Rose, a young romantic; the tales spun for Violet by her Grand Momma, who communicates with the Virgin Mary and daily with her dead son's ghost; and the memories of Frank Cardinal, a 'damaged' addict who searches for solace in dreams of Rose and Kamloops. As well, the play owes much to my love of old film. I was influenced by the rather overblown styles of early silent movies, Film Noir, and old gangster movies.

Where indicated in dialogue, '/' means speakers overlap, '-' means the next speaker picks up right away, and '...' means that actors are reacting without dialogue.

Act I

Scene 1

Darkness. Sound of a train approaching. Dim lights up on the Red Dragon; it is night. Seen in shadow on the train are: MOMMA, JOHNNY, BIG MAN, and 'ROSE'. 'ROSE' has a red suitcase with her. The train picks up speed, begins to lose control, brakes scream. The train lurches and the people on board shout: 'Help!', 'Rosie!', 'Shannon!', 'Momma!', 'Johnny!' An explosion and bodies lurch and fall. The train smokes, sighs, wheezes like a slain dragon. It is dying and so are the people on board. Limbs emerge and struggle then disappear back into the rubble. Then a momentary silence, except for the train itself, which continues to shudder. From a dark area of the stage: the tapping of typewriter keys, quickly at first and then losing momentum; a pause. VIOLET lights a cigarette and, as she does, her face is revealed. Stage lights slowly rise to expose VIOLET in her entirety: a young woman smartly outfitted in the style of 1949. She considers what she has written: the train crash and the wreckage on stage. She types again briefly and a survivor—a woman: 'ROSE'—rises slowly and emerges from the wreck: shadowy, dark, illusive and anonymous in the grey smoke and night. She surveys the area—for other survivors? witnesses?—and then begins to walk off into the darkness. VIOLET watches. Dissatisfied with the shape of her story, she begins to type again. Her typing stops 'ROSE'. She returns to the wreck,

> *picks up her red suitcase and then vanishes into the night. VIOLET watches, then rips a sheet of paper from the typewriter carriage. She crumples the paper up slowly. As she does so, the lights fade on the wreck. Lights fade to black on VIOLET as she watches the wreck lose definition. Its shadowy bulk continues to loom in the background throughout the play.*

Scene 2

> *A rainy evening, 1949. Sounds of a train entering a Vancouver train station and coming to rest. MOMMA and JOHNNY lurk upstage in shadow, waiting, watching. They are incognito, unobserved by FRANK CARDINAL or, later, VIOLET. CARDINAL enters, limping, and carrying the red suitcase. He waits. VIOLET enters. Seeing her, CARDINAL simply stares. VIOLET crosses to him.*

VIOLET: Mr. Cardinal?

CARDINAL: …

VIOLET: Well…

> *He hands her the red bag.*

You're sure it's hers?

CARDINAL: …

VIOLET: You have no idea who sent it?

CARDINAL: …

VIOLET: Help me.

CARDINAL: None.

VIOLET: How did you know my mother?

CARDINAL: Her parents. They raised me like I was their own.

VIOLET: My grandparents?! Where are they now?

CARDINAL: Passed away.

VIOLET: When?

CARDINAL: Nine years ago.

VIOLET: Nine years! Why wasn't I told?!

CARDINAL: There's a lot of history here, Miss Bigillini.

VIOLET: And it's mine. Who sent this? What's in it?

CARDINAL: I don't know.

VIOLET: Wasn't it wrapped? Wasn't it addressed to me? Care of you?

CARDINAL: ...

VIOLET: People walked away from that crash. Didn't they? Didn't they?!

CARDINAL: Three.

VIOLET: We know of. Because they came back. Right?

CARDINAL: ...

VIOLET: Someone had this all these years. Someone who knew where I was. Someone who knew where you were.

CARDINAL: ...

VIOLET: Say something!

CARDINAL: Look, kid, Lucy is probably—

VIOLET: I'm gonna find her!

She begins to exit with the bag.

CARDINAL: Miss Bigillini.

Hands her his card.

VIOLET: *(Reading.)* Inspector Frank Cardinal of the Canadian Pacific Railway. You're a railway cop?

CARDINAL: If you need to talk…

VIOLET: Ha! Wish me luck, Inspector.

She exits. CARDINAL watches her until she disappears. He removes a toy train from his pocket and runs it lightly up the underside of his wrist. He shivers. MOMMA and JOHNNY are watching. Lights fade on CARDINAL, cross fade to…

Scene 3

MOMMA, evening of the same day. She enters the vault containing SHANNON's tomb.

MOMMA: She's here. Arrived today on the train from California. The Cardinal met her. Gave her a small, red bag. Whad'ya think? Are we ready for this, Baby?

As if in answer, a Puccini aria begins to rise from the tomb and Shannon's 'ghost' appears to MOMMA in dim light. He is barely there, exists only in MOMMA's mind. MOMMA, delighted that he has joined her, crosses herself and begins to pray.

Scene 4

Later the same night in her hotel room. VIOLET opens her mother's suitcase and begins to unpack and examine every item. She pulls a black overcoat out of the suitcase, buries her nose in it. Finds a crucifix.

VIOLET: One wooden crucifix. He's lost two toes.

*She puts the crucifix on then finds a formal portrait
of a middle aged couple.*

(*Reading.*) Daniel and Violet Plant, 1922, Kamloops,
B.C. Grandma and Grandpa.

*She places the photograph where she can see it
clearly. Finds a pair of black pumps and slips them
on.*

A perfect fit!

*From the case she pulls lingerie including a black
slip embroidered with tiny, red roses.*

Ooh la la! Tiny, red roses.

*She finds a red leather belt, a Bible, and, finally, a
little black book: LUCY's diary.*

What's this?

*She opens the book to the inside front page and
reads.*

May 1st, 1923. This diary is the personal and
confidential property of the next Miss Lillian Gish.
Intruders, if caught, will be prosecuted,
persecuted, and, finally, executed.

Hallelujah!

Dear Diary, I'm packed and ready to go. Couldn't
sleep, too nervous. Mummy kept on at me '...to eat
my potatoes, drink my milk. Sit down, Darling.
You got ants in your pants?' Poor Mummy. Father,
well he just kept his head buried in that damned
seed catalogue, shoving mountains of mashed
spuds in his face like there was no tomorrow. Sure
glad Frankie's in Edmonton. That boy always
could read me.

*Light shift and VIOLET 'becomes' LUCY. She
closes the suitcase and slips her mother's coat on.*

LUCY: So Dearest Diary, you and I are blowing the dust
                 from this dump right off our behinds. Tomorrow
                 morning, first train out! What am I
                 saying...morning has risen! Yikes! First stop
                 Vancouver. I'll take care of 'things' there and, then,
                 after I've made some dough...Hollywood,
                 California here I come.

CONDUCTOR: *(Off.)* All aboard!

Scene 5

                 LUCY steps downstage and the Kamloops train
                 station comes to life around her. Lights settle into
                 this new reality and the sounds of trains and a small
                 crowd hustling on a platform usher us into the
                 world of LUCY's diary. It is May 2, 1923. Unseen
                 by LUCY, BIG MAN watches as she puts her ticket
                 in her bra for safekeeping. She turns and bumps into
                 him.

LUCY: Oh! Excuse me. I'm so sorry.

BIG MAN: Don't be.

LUCY: Um, can you tell me, please, is this the train to
                 Vancouver?

BIG MAN: Leavin' in five minutes.

LUCY: Thank you.

BIG MAN: Don't mention it, Doll.

                 Flustered and excited, LUCY turns as BIG MAN
                 tips his hat. He scoops up her bag and exits. LUCY
                 doesn't see her bag walking away.

LUCY: Doll?! Me oh my.

                 Enter CARDINAL running.

CARDINAL: Lucy! Thank God.

LUCY: What are you doing here?!

CARDINAL: Me?! Mum's in a panic about you.

LUCY: You're supposed to be in Edmonton.

CARDINAL: And you're supposed to be at home.

LUCY: When did you become such a pompous pain in the neck, Frank Cardinal?

CARDINAL: Let's go. Where's your bag?

LUCY: My bag? Oh no! He couldn't have.

CARDINAL: Who?

LUCY: He must have. That man stole my bag!

CARDINAL: Description?

LUCY: Red leather. You know the one.

CARDINAL: The man?

LUCY: Oh...big...strong face like, like William S. Hart. Devilish.

CARDINAL: William Who?

LUCY: The actor, Bonehead.

CARDINAL: Specifics.

LUCY: Lots of big, white teeth, sideburns...and eyes...

CARDINAL: Christ!

LUCY: Mesmerizing.

CARDINAL: Which way did he go? Sit.

LUCY: But...

              He exits, running.

              Be careful!

The train is gearing up to go. CARDINAL returns with her bag.

LUCY: My hero! Where was it?

CARDINAL: Gents' lavatory. Check the contents.

LUCY: My money! Every cent. How could he?

CARDINAL: Anything else?

LUCY: His hands, they were all over my personal possessions. Imagine that. Fingering my panties.

CARDINAL: Let's get you home.

LUCY: Oh no you don't.

CONDUCTOR: *(Off.)* Canadian Pacific Railway Train bound for Vancouver, with all stops along the way, leaving now from Platform One. All aboard!

LUCY: An ounce of prevention. *(She pulls ticket and some cash from her bra.)*

CARDINAL: You're distraught.

LUCY: Frankie, just kiss me goodbye. Whoa! That is not the kind of kiss I had in mind.

CARDINAL: Again.

LUCY: I'm serious, this, that, it's over between us!

CARDINAL: Marry me.

LUCY: I'm not ready to settle down. You know that!

CARDINAL: Marry me.

LUCY: I'd drive you to drink in a week.

CARDINAL: Marry me!

LUCY: Alright, you'd drive me to drink in a week!

CARDINAL: Luce (pronounced 'Loose'), you're not getting on that train.

LUCY: I'll scream and…say you tried to steal my bag!

CARDINAL: Sweetheart, they'll never believe you. I'm an Inspector /of the Canadian

LUCY: /I don't care if you're Jesus Christ! And if you tell Mummy and Daddy, I'll never talk to you again. Look, I'll let them know where I am as soon as I get there. Aw, Frankie, please.

CARDINAL moves aside.

CARDINAL: Where can I find you?

LUCY: Bless you!

LUCY boards the train. Lighting shift as the train moves off slowly.

CARDINAL: If that man's on the train, don't talk to him. Here…take the crucifix.

He begins to fumble at a crucifix hanging on a chain around his neck.

LUCY: No time!

CARDINAL: Wait!

LUCY: I'll write.

CARDINAL: As soon as you get to…Vancouver?

LUCY: Love you!

CARDINAL: As soon as you get to Vancouver!

Inside train. LUCY moves to compartment.

LUCY: Phew!

Enter BIG MAN.

BIG MAN: May I?

LUCY: You! Leave me alone. I mean it! I'll scream!

BIG MAN: I won't bite.

LUCY: Aaaaaaah!

BIG MAN: Relax! I just thought we could be friends.

LUCY: Where's my money? I could have missed my train on account of you.

BIG MAN: Nah! You hid your ticket in your bosoms.

LUCY: Get out of my way!

BIG MAN: I'm sorry, I couldn't help noticin'. Look! I'm on my knees here.

LUCY: Get up! You look ridiculous. Oh dear, somebody reconsiders, decides to make it up, and what do I do? Bite his head off. Well, I didn't exactly bite off your head, but...you've still got my money!

BIG MAN: You travellin' with anyone? Your husband, a boyfriend?

LUCY: Yes! My...brother, if you must know. And he'll be here any moment.

BIG MAN: Your brother? Close family, eh? *(Makes smooching noise.)*

LUCY: You don't scare me, Mister. I'm going straight to the authorities.

BIG MAN: Now that's not nice.

LUCY: *(About to leave.)* Excuse me.

             He returns her money.

BIG MAN: Forgive me, Doll, for I have sinned.

LUCY: Is it all here?! That'll be one hundred Rosaries and a billion Hail Marys. Turn around. Do it!

               She hides her money in her bra. He finds a moment to look without her seeing.

BIG MAN: Catholic? Me, I'm lapsed.

LUCY: I'll say. To tell you the truth, I think I'm lapsing myself. You can look now. Don't get me wrong. I believe, and I know Our Lord Jesus and the Blessed Virgin are with me. And, by the way, She's watching over me right now, so don't you get any funny ideas.

BIG MAN: Yes, Ma'am.

LUCY: But I also know that He had time for Mary Magdalen and thieves and a whole host of wild characters. Right? Anyway, how can it matter if you're really good if it's all you've ever known? What am I doing?! And what's so darned funny anyway? Well, it's been…interesting, but I'll be on my way now.

BIG MAN: Ya been in Vancouver before? Rough city. I can get ya a room at my Momma's place. She runs a clean joint, interesting clientele, great grub.

               (Tempting.) A cast of wild characters.

LUCY: Who are you?

BIG MAN: A business executive, friends call me The Big Man.

LUCY: $86.00 is a pathetic haul, Mr. Big.

BIG MAN: I liked what I saw and I invested.

LUCY: Oh.

BIG MAN: Won't ya take a seat?

LUCY: I don't think so, thank you.

BIG MAN: Oh...I get it

LUCY: What?

BIG MAN: You are afraid.

LUCY: Don't flatter yourself.

              She sits.

              So, uh, what kind of business are you in?

BIG MAN: I dabble in a number of enterprises: clubs,
              restaurants, the like. My name is ...aw, what the
              hell, Shannon Bigillini, but, like I said, friends call
              me-

LUCY: Shannon? Isn't that a girl's/name?

BIG MAN: /It ain't no girl's name!

LUCY: If you say so.

BIG MAN: I do. You? Your name?

LUCY: Rose...Wood.

              *Text refers to LUCY as ROSE for the rest of the
              script except in CARDINAL's memories and other
              places where LUCY is the logical choice.*

BIG MAN: Pleased to meet ya, Rose Wood. Drink?

              Produces a flask.

ROSE: Is that straight alcohol?! No, thank you, really, I
              couldn't.

BIG MAN: *(Tempting.)* Adventure. Suit yourself, Doll. Hey, I
              got just the thing. One exotic cocktail comin' right
              up.

              *With the flourish of a magician, BIG MAN pulls a
              tiny 'bar' out of his case and begins to mix her a
              drink. There's an image of a red dragon on the side of
              his cocktail shaker.*

ROSE: Is that a dragon?

BIG MAN: A little advertising for a new venture I'm involved in…a private and very exclusive club: The Red Dragon.

ROSE: What is this?

BIG MAN: *(Name of drink.)* Dragon's Fire. A jigger of this, a dash of that, a shot of mystery, and stir.

ROSE: Sounds dangerous.

               She bolts it and wants another drink.

               May I?

BIG MAN: You betcha.

               Pours another drink.

ROSE: So where would I be staying? I mean where is Momma's place?

BIG MAN: It's a little boardin' house on the edge of Chinatown.

ROSE: Chinatown! Did you see *Broken Blossoms*? Starring Lillian Gish?

BIG MAN: 'Fraid I don't get out to the pictures much.

ROSE: Oh, but you must! D. W. Griffith, the director, is a genius. Lillian plays… an innocent. Her father, a drunkard and a boxer—the great Battling Burrows—beats her. Constantly! But one day he goes too far. Lillian flees and she's rescued by a Chinaman, an opium addict. But this addict is her friend, an angel of mercy. Oh, he's a man alright, and he has his thoughts, if you know what I mean. But he's a good person, and he falls for Lillian…hook, line and sinker. Naturally, it ends badly.

BIG MAN: Naturally. What happens?

ROSE: Her father beats her to death.

BIG MAN: And the Chink? Pardon me. The uh…Angel?

ROSE: Stabs himself, right in the heart.

BIG MAN: Jesus!

ROSE: Love. Oh…look! Where are we?

BIG MAN: That's the Fraser.

ROSE: Still? The mighty Fraser. It must have been something alright being Mr. Simon Fraser.

BIG MAN: Where ya been all my life?

ROSE: Kamloops. Well, just outside. Imagine, travelling down that river in canoes. This is my very first time going anywhere. What must it have been like for Fraser? Seeing all of this for the first time. Do you think there were women with him?

BIG MAN: Why not?

ROSE: They're never in the history books. I'll tell you a secret, but you've gotta tell one, too.

BIG MAN: Shoot.

He pours the rest of the drink in her glass.

ROSE: I'm running away.

BIG MAN: Ya don't say.

ROSE: To Hollywood. Vancouver's just the first stop. I'm going to make history.

BIG MAN: You an actress?

ROSE: Uh huh. Or maybe a writer.

BIG MAN: You're pretty enough to be in the pictures.

ROSE: Your turn.

BIG MAN: I cook.

ROSE: That's it?

BIG MAN: Nah. I'm learnin' to do magic with food. My first memories are of Momma's kitchen: big steam bath of a room: black and red checkerboard tile, copper pots, choppin' block, and killer knives everywhere.

ROSE: You've got a way with words.

She gets her diary and pen out.

May I? I'm recording all my really interesting experiences. For posterity.

BIG MAN: Posterity? Until I say 'no more', eh, then it's off the record.

ROSE: Off the record.

BIG MAN: Man, that's one crazy broad. Meat mallets, wooden spoons, rollin' pins…one time, and this is no lie, a cleaver. Flung it at me and it stuck in the choppin' block.

ROSE: Your mother?!

BIG MAN: She's an artist, temperamental. But sometimes she gets softer when she's on a roll, shaping a masterpiece. She gets soft, hot, and generous. My secret desire, Rose Wood, is to cook a ten course meal: big, meaty food. I serve it to Momma: a surprise. Watch those little beads of sweat sprinkle her upper lip as she unfolds. I feed her like a baby, gently push it in. It slides down her warm, wet throat. She sings my praises. Hell, we sing together. Puccini. Yeah. Giacomo Antonio Domenico Michele Secondo Maria Puccini.

He bursts briefly into song.

ROSE: Wow!

BIG MAN: You like opera?

ROSE: 'Fraid I don't get out to the opera much.

BIG MAN: Oh, but you…will. Lose the book now. We toast one another with a little sambucca, and then Momma signs her enterprises, lock, stock, and barrel, over to me. We seal it with a smoke and a kiss. Then I send her straight to heaven. Or hell.

ROSE: What?!

BIG MAN: Nah, seriously, I've just got this desire, see? To cook for people I care about. Watch them enjoy the fruits of my labour. Maybe I could, uh, prepare somethin' special for you one night.

ROSE: Holy doodle.

Scene 6

The Diary continues. It is early evening of the day ROSE left Kamloops. JOHNNY is blindfolded and on his knees in MOMMA's kitchen. MOMMA threatens him with a 'killer knife'.

MOMMA: Can Johnny come out to play?

JOHNNY howls like a wolf. Perhaps MOMMA does, too. Enter BIG MAN and ROSE.

BIG MAN: Momma, I'm home. Jesus Christ!

MOMMA smacks him.

MOMMA: Enough!

BIG MAN: Ow!

MOMMA: Sorry, Miss. But, as Shannon very well knows, I don't like people takin' our Lord's name in vain. Ya have a good trip, Son?

BIG MAN: The best.

Quietly, he speaks to MOMMA.

Here's the dough. Old Man Lee says he's lookin' forward to the next shipment of-

MOMMA:	Grazie. Now button it.
BIG MAN:	Momma, Johnny...Miss Rose Wood.
ROSE:	Hello, Mrs. Bigellini. Mr. Johnny.
MOMMA:	Call me Momma. Everyone does.
JOHNNY:	Ya can call me Johnny.
BIG MAN:	I thought maybe she could rent the little room upstairs, Momma.
MOMMA:	I let it out this mornin'.
BIG MAN:	Damn. I'm sorry, Rosie.
MOMMA:	Wait a minute. There's a small, and I do mean small, sleepin' compartment available on the Dragon.
ROSE:	The railway club?
MOMMA:	Ya know about that? My, my, my, what a big mouth you have, Shannon.
ROSE:	Um, I was really hoping to live in Vancouver.
MOMMA:	So?
ROSE:	Well, don't trains move?
JOHNNY:	She's no dummy.
BIG MAN:	The Dragon's stationed in the railway yards, Rosie, unless Momma gets a special contract. Then we'll hook her up, eh Momma? Can't wait! Rosie's from Kamloops. New in town, lookin' for work.
MOMMA:	Ya don't say? Turn around, Rosa. Legs please.

ROSE: I beg your pardon?

JOHNNY: Here, let me help.

                  He pulls her skirt up.

MOMMA: Not bad.

BIG MAN: /Butt out, Johnny!

ROSE: /Do you mind?!

MOMMA: Relax!

BIG MAN: Rosie's a good girl, Momma. Capiche?

MOMMA: Sure. What'ya know about cards?

ROSE: Um, cribbage, solitaire. I was never much good at
                  Bridge.

MOMMA: Black Jack? Roulette? Can ya deal?

ROSE: I'm a fast learner.

BIG MAN: I'll teach her.

JOHNNY: You?

BIG MAN: What's so damned funny?

MOMMA: Not a thing, Shannon.

                  (To JOHNNY.) Not a thing. So, what'ya think about
                  Rosa here, Johnny?

JOHNNY: Tasty.

MOMMA: You've got yourself a job and a place to stay, little
                  girl.

ROSE: Oh…thank you! You won't regret it.

MOMMA: Yeah, yeah. We'll talk details tomorrow. Pick up
                  the girl's bag, Shannon!

BIG MAN: Way ahead of ya, Momma. Miss Wood? After you.

ROSE: Gosh! Good bye Momma, Johnny.

                 Exit ROSE and BIG MAN.

MOMMA: Now, where were we?

                 *JOHNNY howls like a wolf. Perhaps she joins in.
                 They freeze as lights find VIOLET in her hotel room
                 in 1949. She is reading ROSE's diary.*

VIOLET: *(Reads as MOMMA.)* Now, where were we? *(Reads
                 ROSE's description.)* As we were leaving, the man
                 named Johnny began to howl like a wolf again and
                 Shannon's Momma—

                 She turns the page. The rest of the book is blank.

                 Damn! Damn you!

                 *She slams the book shut and lights snap out on
                 MOMMA and JOHNNY. VIOLET checks the bag
                 again for possible hiding places. She finds nothing.
                 She retrieves CARDINAL's card, picks up the
                 telephone and dials.*

Scene 7

                 *Lights stay up on VIOLET and with the ring of the
                 telephone rise on CARDINAL in his home. He has
                 been smoking opium and the pipe and the little train
                 are nearby.*

CARDINAL: H'llo.

VIOLET: I need to talk to you. Now. Face to face.

CARDINAL: …

VIOLET: Inspector Cardinal?

CARDINAL: …

VIOLET: Please.

CARDINAL: 1436 Newson Street, apartment 2.

Lights down on VIOLET as she hangs up.

Where are you taking me this time, Luce?

Lights shift as we move into CARDINAL's memory. Location: train tracks in countryside outside Kamloops on a hot summer's day, 1923. LUCY enters and stands on the tracks, arms outstretched. She is barefoot. CARDINAL, as YOUNG FRANK, enters his memory.

FRANK: Lucy?

LUCY: Shhh! It's coming, Silly. I can feel it through the soles of my feet. Close your eyes.

They both stand on the tracks, one in front of the other, with their arms outstretched and eyes closed, waiting and listening for the train. Sounds of a baking hot day in the interior of British Columbia: bugs, birds, a dry wind, and then, almost imperceptibly, a train whistle far off in the distance. The sound of the approaching train builds slowly during this memory until it screams past at the end of the scene.

FRANK: There!

LUCY: Mmm, I love that sound.

FRANK: Luce, I—

She produces bottle of hooch.

LUCY: Surprise! Let's get snozzled! Congratulations on your promotion, Inspector Cardinal.

A toast: she drinks. They pass the bottle back and forth.

Whew! Burns. All the way down to my gizzard. Gizzzzzzzard. What words do you love?

FRANK: 'Snozzled'. 'Promotion'. I'm scared.

LUCY: You'll be great.

FRANK: Are you...?

LUCY: Am I...?

FRANK: Gonna be here when I come home?

LUCY: From Edmonton? Honestly? I hope not.

            He grabs her.

FRANK: Promise me you'll write and let me know where you are.

LUCY: That hurts!

FRANK: Promise.

LUCY: Cross my heart.

FRANK: And promise...

            She giggles.

            What?! What's so damned funny?

LUCY: Your face is turning all blotchy and red.

FRANK: You really shouldn't drink, Miss Plant.

LUCY: *(Bad French accent.)* And why ze hell not, Monsieur Cardinal?

FRANK: You can't hold the stuff.

LUCY: Pphhh! And you can?!

FRANK: Nope. Weaklings, the pair of us.

LUCY: France! Perhaps I'll go zere. Sink of it...Notre Dame, ze Seine, ze Latin Quarter, and, oh, ze men!—

FRANK: Stop it! Don't you understand? I can't, I won't live without you—

LUCY: Shhh. Shhh. Jeez, Cardinal, I don't even want to go to France.

              Takes a crucifix from around her neck and puts it around his.

              A loan. I want it back, OK? When you get home.

FRANK: I'm gonna take care of you.

LUCY: Oh, Frankie, aim higher.

FRANK: We'll cross Canada together. On the train. Whoo! Whoo!

LUCY: You and your crazy train fetish.

FRANK: Me?

LUCY: I'm just jealous. They pass through this dump just long enough to pick up passengers and then, poof!

FRANK: What have you got against paradise?

LUCY: See that cloud? What's it look like to you?

FRANK: A dragon.

LUCY: It's breathing fire! And there's Saint George. See?

FRANK: Where?

LUCY: The little guy under the dragon's belly. He's pulled his sword. Oops! Now you see him, now you don't. What are you doing?

              He stares at her.

              Take a picture, why don't you?

FRANK: You've changed.

LUCY: Close your eyes. Do it. Now give me your hands.

Come on.

> *She places them on her breasts. They have never done this before.*

FRANK: Luce…

LUCY: It's coming! Can you feel it now?

FRANK: Let's go.

LUCY: Here!

FRANK: The grass is longer over there.

LUCY: The earth is jumping.

FRANK: They'll see.

LUCY: Right here.

> *She pulls him into an embrace as the train roars past them. Lights down on them and sound and lights to suggest a long train passing, passing, passing… Lights shift back to the reality of FRANK's room in 1949 where he has surrendered to his memory. He begins to unbutton his trousers. A loud and insistent knocking at the door shocks him out of his 'reverie' and onto his feet.*

FRANK: Coming!

> *He pulls himself together, hides the little train and the opium pipe. VIOLET is at the door. She enters carrying an umbrella and wearing ROSE's pumps. Lights and focus shift as…*

Scene 8

Phone rings. MOMMA, isolated in light, answers.

MOMMA: Yeah?

Another light isolates JOHNNY in a phone booth.

JOHNNY: She's in Cardinal's apartment. Just arrived.

MOMMA: The bag?

JOHNNY: Nope.

MOMMA: Where exactly are ya?

JOHNNY: Phone booth across from the main entrance to his building. I can see them pretty clearly.

MOMMA: Anything interestin' happenin'?

JOHNNY: Not yet.

MOMMA: You stay put until she comes out.

JOHNNY: In which case I follows her. Right?

MOMMA: Good boy.

She hangs up and lights fade out on MOMMA leaving JOHNNY in the shadow as…

Scene 9

Focus shifts back to CARDINAL and VIOLET.

VIOLET: Her diary.

He takes the book and begins to read, hungrily skimming through the pages.

I'm just about crazy for a stiff drink. Got anything? Scotch?

CARDINAL: …

VIOLET: *(Digging for cigarettes.)* Gotta light?

CARDINAL: …

VIOLET: No bad habits?

CARDINAL: Do you want me to read this?

CARDINAL reads.

VIOLET: What were my grandparents like?

CARDINAL: Decent folk.

VIOLET: Truly, Inspector, you are a fountain of information.

CARDINAL: He was a farmer. She was a farmer's wife. They worked hard. We never went without.

VIOLET: But my Mother was unhappy there. And it looks like she got off that train and went straight to Grand Momma's place with a complete stranger. Did you know my father?

CARDINAL: You talked to Momma yet?

VIOLET: Can't you just give me one straight answer?!

CARDINAL: …

VIOLET: She doesn't know I'm here.

CARDINAL: I wouldn't count on that.

VIOLET: Yeah, well… I don't believe even half of what she's written. Grand Momma and Johnny Jones?! Fiction.

CARDINAL: Go see her.

VIOLET: There's a Bible. It's inscribed: 'To Rosa with love from M'. But then you probably knew that already.

CARDINAL: Ask her about the other diary.

VIOLET: What?!

CARDINAL: Red leather, gold embossing. Real smart looking book.

VIOLET: Jesus! What the hell else should I know?

CARDINAL: It's late, Kid.

VIOLET: This is my story. You understand? Mine.

CARDINAL: Ask her about the Dragon.

VIOLET: The Red Dragon?

CARDINAL: Ask her what she was selling.

VIOLET: What's that got to do with my mother?

CARDINAL: I'll call you a cab.

VIOLET: Damn you! I'll walk.

             He notices her shoes.

CARDINAL: Her shoes.

             Unable to stop himself, he makes a move to stroke a shoe.

             I'll walk you to your hotel.

VIOLET: No! Thank you. Good night, Inspector Cardinal.

             Lights down on CARDINAL's room and up on the street. It is raining. VIOLET begins to exit. She senses someone following, and turns. JOHNNY ducks out of sight. CARDINAL, watching JOHNNY watching VIOLET, then ducks out of his line of vision. VIOLET sees nobody. She exits. JOHNNY follows her at a discreet distance. CARDINAL tails JOHNNY.

Scene 10

VIOLET's hotel room later that evening. MOMMA has been rifling through the red suitcase and is now repairing a portion of lining with a needle and thread. There are some papers beside her. She removed these pages from a diary which had been, and is, once again, hidden behind the lining of the suitcase. MOMMA closes the red suitcase and puts the papers in her purse. Enter VIOLET.

VIOLET: Oh!

MOMMA: Hello Violet.

VIOLET: What are you doing here?

MOMMA: Visitin' my only grandchild. Were ya plannin' on callin' me any time soon?

VIOLET: Of course. How did you get into my room?

MOMMA: I can be a very persuasive woman. You're lookin' stylish.

VIOLET: I can afford the best. Thanks to you.

MOMMA: California treatin' ya OK?

VIOLET: California is a dream. Do you recognize this bag?

MOMMA: That's it? 'California is a dream? Do you recognize this bag?' No 'How are ya, Grand Momma? It's good to see ya? I missed ya?' Where's my hug?

VIOLET hugs her.

VIOLET: How are 'ya', Grand Momma?

MOMMA: Better...now. You losin' weight, Sweet Pea?

VIOLET: No.

MOMMA: I'll cook lunch for ya tomorrow. Ya workin' with any big stars yet? Joan Crawford? Betty Davis?

VIOLET: I'm a junior writer. There are hundreds of us. I saw Humphrey Bogart though.

MOMMA: Yeah? Now that's a man I'd like to cook for. So... 'The Cardinal' still carryin' a torch for Rosa?

VIOLET: Why didn't you tell me about him?

MOMMA: What's to tell?

VIOLET: And what about my grandparents in Kamloops?

MOMMA: Ya think it was easy for me, little girl? I held my son's body in my arms that day. There was a hole where his face shoulda bin. Maybe I made some mistakes, but I made damned good and sure I kept his baby girl safe. Big adjustments all around. For you.

VIOLET: So you recognize the suitcase?

MOMMA: Sure.

VIOLET: What about this Bible? 'M'. That you?

MOMMA: You bet. An engagement present.

VIOLET: Would you recognize my mother's diary if you saw it?

MOMMA: Why? Was it in the bag, too?

VIOLET: No.

MOMMA: Rosa was always scribblin' in that book. Watchin' and scribblin'. Gave me the heebie jeebies.

VIOLET: I do that, too.

MOMMA: You're my girl.

VIOLET: Can you describe it? The diary?

MOMMA: What for?

VIOLET: Please.

MOMMA: Okay, uh, red leather. The kid loved red. It was a
                gift from your Poppa. Rosie. He called her Rosie.
                Rosie this, Rosie that, how Rosie was so special.
                And how Rosie was writin' for keeps. History.

VIOLET: Posterity.

MOMMA: Bingo. The best damned book his Momma's money
                could buy.

VIOLET: Not like this one.

                Produces ROSE's diary.

MOMMA: Let me see that!

                MOMMA begins to scan the journal.

VIOLET: The entries take me right up to her arrival in
                Vancouver, just after she met you.

MOMMA: So?

VIOLET: You and Johnny Jones?!

MOMMA: So?

VIOLET: In the kitchen? With knives?!

MOMMA: You believe that shit?

VIOLET: What happened to my mother after she met
                Poppa?

MOMMA: Ya know what happened.

VIOLET: I know what you told me. It's not enough.

MOMMA: Baby, Rosa came to Vancouver with nothin'. She
                married Shannon, played hard and got a lot of
                beautiful things, gave birth to you—best thing she
                ever did—and got mixed up with a lot of bad shit.
                Your mother fucked up—forgive me—broke your
                Poppa's heart and died when the Red Dragon
                exploded. End of story.

VIOLET: You survived. Johnny survived. People walked
               away from the wreck.

MOMMA: Ya wanna believe your mother walked out on ya?
               Even a cat don't leave her kittens. Come home with
               me. Sleep late in your own bed and I'll make ya a
               beautiful lunch.

VIOLET: Did you read the other diary?

MOMMA: I did not.

VIOLET: Do you know where it is?

MOMMA: *(A lie.)* I do not.

VIOLET: Cross your heart?

MOMMA: Cross my heart.

VIOLET: Mine, too.

> *This is an important ritual of theirs. MOMMA
> violates it now. She crosses her heart then takes
> VIOLET's hand and crosses VIOLET's heart.
> MOMMA kisses her granddaughter's palm.*

MOMMA: Ya comin' home?

VIOLET: I'm sleeping here. Why did you hate my mother?

MOMMA: Little girl...

VIOLET: I'm not a little girl!

MOMMA: Rosa, bless her, was a grenade waitin' to explode.
               Soon as I set eyes on her pretty face I could see that.
               Shannon was my baby, Violet. Ya comin' for lunch
               today?

VIOLET: I'm her baby. Please.

MOMMA: ...

VIOLET: I'm writing it. Setting it down in black and white.
               With or without your help.

MOMMA: A movie?!

VIOLET: For posterity.

MOMMA: The world don't need to know our business.

VIOLET: I do. I'm all grown up now. Tell me about the Red Dragon. What you were selling.

MOMMA: Cardinal! What'd that little bastard tell 'ya?

VIOLET: …

MOMMA: I'll make ya a deal. Get into that bed of yours and I'll tell ya a story.

VIOLET: The story.

MOMMA: Sure.

> *VIOLET slips under the covers and waits for her story. MOMMA tucks her in as she begins.*

Once upon a time… First off, I wasn't always the way ya see me now, Sweet Pea. Ya gotta understand. I was a young woman on my own. Good-For-Nothin'-Husband, bless him, overdosed and left me stranded with your Poppa. He wasn't even eight years old. What skills did I have? I could cook and I was a looker. What connections did I have? The low-life scum your Grand Poppa bottomed out with. It was a place to start. In a couple a years I was doin' OK. Fingers in lots of pies, some of them rotten. And, God forgive me, I formed some unusual romantic attachments. And I wasn't always a good Momma to your father. There, I said it. But I been doin' penance for a lot of years, and he and me, we're like this now. *(Gestures they're 'tight'.)* And Shannon's singin' again, Violet. Like an angel. What am I talkin' about? My boy is an angel and he's singin'. Ya should of heard him cut loose when I told him ya were here.

VIOLET: Grand Momma please…

MOMMA: Ya sure you're ready for this?

VIOLET: Yes!

MOMMA: Well, don't say I didn't warn ya.

VIOLET: Nothing you can say or do at this point is going to
            shock me.

MOMMA: Rosa was sharp. She went to work on your Poppa
            first thing.

> *Shift as BIG MAN enters MOMMA's story
> singing Puccini and carrying a tray of oysters. He
> prepares for an intimate dinner as MOMMA and
> VIOLET watch.*

But Johnny and me, we had our eyes on her.

> *JOHNNY enters the story and takes his place to
> watch BIG MAN and ROSE.*

Scene 11

> *MOMMA's story. MOMMA's kitchen. The year is
> 1923. BIG MAN is preparing a meal and singing
> Puccini. ROSE enters. She is a lovely and
> precocious 'Alice', dressed simply in a white dress.*

BIG MAN: Miss Alice I presume.

ROSE: You did say oysters.

BIG MAN: To die for.

> *BIG MAN pulls out a chair for her, unfolds her
> serviette, etc.*

ROSE: Gosh! Shouldn't Momma be sitting here?

BIG MAN: Yeah, well, tonight I'd like to barbecue the old
            buzzard.

ROSE: Why?!

BIG MAN: Johnny Jones.

ROSE: The wolf man.

BIG MAN: Me, her own flesh and blood, she humiliates in front of the whole damned crew. I'm tellin' ya, this time she's gone too far.

ROSE: What happened?

BIG MAN: Nah. Not tonight. Open up, Alice.

He begins to feed her wine and oysters.

VIOLET: Wait a minute!

Story action freezes. VIOLET breaks out of tableau.

MOMMA: What?!

VIOLET: 'She's gone too far.' What did you do?

MOMMA: Beats me.

VIOLET: I'm not buying.

MOMMA: Alright, already, but we're comin' back to this. Alice in Wonderland, my ass.

Shift. MOMMA enters the story. The time is earlier on the day of the oyster dinner. MOMMA addresses her 'gang'.

Alright all of youse, listen up. The Red Dragon is ready to roll! And she's a work of art, a creature of beauty! Finest interior detailin' money can buy: black and red leather, mahogany, etched glass, marble counters, red velvet curtains. Let the games begin!

Sound of applause, cheers from 'The Gang'.

Thank you! Thank you very much! Naturally, you are all invited, make that expected, at the openin' of the Red Dragon. For those of you who are just now comin' up to speed on this particular venture, I gotta deal happenin' with a certain enterprisin' politician. We're covered: legal stuff, security matters, transportation concerns. As always in our establishments, there'll be gamblin', fine dinin',...

BIG MAN: The finest!

MOMMA: Grazie, Son. And booze. And behind the scenes, for our members with, shall we say, more exotic tastes...The Dragon's Fire. In these small, private compartments, the more 'discriminatin' members will be able to get...

> *MOMMA hesitates and then stops. She breaks out of the story reality.*

I'm not sure this is such a good idea, Violet. How 'bout we call it a night? We can talk tomorrow.

VIOLET: Fine. You go home and I'll go back to see Mr. Cardinal.

MOMMA: Baby... I'd undo the past. If I could.

VIOLET: Just tell me the truth.

> *MOMMA moves back into the story. At some point during the next speech, VIOLET 'becomes' ROSE and finds an opportunity to move into the story and spy on MOMMA and her gang. She takes her diary with her.*

MOMMA: In these small, private compartments, the more discriminatin' members will be able to get anythin' they want, provided they got the wherewithal. And I do mean anythin', gentlemen: little girls, big girls, boys, if their tastes run that way, privacy, spectator sports, and narcotics. Hell, they can eat it, drink it, smoke it, shoot it, or ride it! Right here in Vancouver or steamin' down the line to their...hearts' desires. Excitin'? Definitely.

Dangerous? Not if we play it wise, which we will. I've got the crew of crews workin' this one, eh? Eh?

Cheers from crew.

Speakin' of which, come on out here and join us, Johnny.

Enter JOHNNY Jones.

JOHNNY: Evenin' Momma, fellas.

MOMMA: Mr. Jones here will be my right hand man on the Dragon.

BIG MAN: Hey, wait a second, Momma! I thought I—

MOMMA: Button it! Where was I? Oh, yeah. Great team, Johnny at the helm. Anythin' strange on the Dragon, aside from the proclivities of our clients, report it to Mr. Jones or me. Naturally, you'll all be workin' hard, keepin' your eyes and ears peeled for trouble, and stayin' sober. Make no mistake…any of you boys so much as lays a finger on our 'merchandise' without my say-so, heads will roll! Right, we're headin' over to The Dragon now. You'll get the full tour and Shannon's gonna give ya the specifics on the openin'.

BIG MAN: I asked ya not to call me that in public.

MOMMA: It's your name, Shannon—

BIG MAN: Jesus.

            MOMMA smacks him.

            Ow!

MOMMA: And if it was good enough for your Grandmother, bless her, it's good enough for you, Shannon.

            JOHNNY has seen ROSE. He whispers to MOMMA to let her know they're being watched.

JOHNNY: All aboard!

> *MOMMA exits to cheers. ROSE comes out of her
> hiding place and JOHNNY surprises her.*

              Lookin' for somethin'?

ROSE: Shannon.

JOHNNY: Been here long?

ROSE: Oh, no. I just got here. Really.

JOHNNY: Give me the book.

ROSE: No! This is my personal diary.

JOHNNY: Not if Momma wants it.

> *He gently runs a knife down the side of her face, her
> neck… She hands him the book. He rips her kitchen
> entry out before returning the book to her.*

              Tasty. I've got my eye on you.

> *ROSE begins to exit.*

Scene 12

> *MOMMA, 1940s, freezes the action of the story.*

MOMMA: So…

> *ROSE and JOHNNY freeze.*

              Back to Wonderland.

> *JOHNNY, ROSE and BIG MAN resume their
> places in the oyster dinner scene. MOMMA is on
> the edge of the action as the story teller.*

> *BIG MAN moves in for a kiss. ROSE avoids.*

ROSE: 'But wait a bit!' the Oysters cried,
               Before we have our 'chat'

For some of us are out of breath,
And all of us are fat!'

BIG MAN: You've barely touched your dinner, Rosie.

                He pursues her. She continues to put him off...a
                tease.

ROSE: Uh, uh, uh, uh...patience is a virtue. And fantasy
                should be served up in tantalizing fragments, one
                dish building on the next.

                She feeds him an oyster.

BIG MAN: What do ya know about fantasy?

ROSE: It's where I live. Do you remember what Humpty
                Dumpty said to Alice?

BIG MAN: Somethin' about eatin' his mushroom.

ROSE: Wrong guy, wrong story.

BIG MAN: Something about eatin' it, and growin' bigger.

ROSE: Holy doodle! Humpty Dumpty was a very big egg.
                He had the King, the Queen, and all their Men at
                his command. A very big egg.

                He pulls her very close.

BIG MAN: What was his secret?

ROSE: Location.

BIG MAN: Mmm.

                She breaks away.

ROSE: And words. He was a smooth operator. It got him
                what he wanted. Cravats, an army, jewels...

BIG MAN: Scrambled.

ROSE: He was an egg. Now, if he and Alice had put
                their...heads together...who knows, he might not

have needed the King, his army, or even his …Momma.

BIG MAN:　　What?

ROSE:　　　I've seen how she treats you. Off with her head!

BIG MAN:　　Jesus.

ROSE:　　　Humiliation…every moment of every day.

BIG MAN:　　Rosie, Baby.

> *He kisses and/or cups his hands over her belly. A moment as he lingers there. The focus on her belly makes her uncomfortable.*

A sweet, ripe, round belly.

ROSE:　　　Down boy!

> *He gets on his hands on knees.*

BIG MAN:　　Woof!

> *ROSE plays MOMMA.*

ROSE:　　　Roll over, Shannon! Again! Ya want an oyster?

> *Offers him one.*

Too damn bad!

> *Pulls the oyster away from him.*

Beg! Now!

> *He does and she rewards him.*

That's Momma's goooood boy.

> *She strokes him, then slaps him.*

BIG MAN:　　Son of a bitch!

ROSE:　　　Off with her head.

BIG MAN: We could use the cleaver.

ROSE: The mallet.

BIG MAN: Kitchen knives!

ROSE: Our bare hands!

BIG MAN: OYSTERS! I'll stuff the old bitch 'til she bursts!

ROSE: Yes!

BIG MAN: Oysters! Oysters! /Oysters! Ohhh Rosie!

ROSE: /Yes! Yes! YES!

> *A sudden transition as VIOLET reacts to the scene above. BIG MAN and JOHNNY freeze.*

VIOLET: Grand MOMMA!

MOMMA: Hey, I'm only reportin' back what Johnny witnessed with his own eyes and ears.

VIOLET: It's disgusting.

MOMMA: You're tellin' me.

VIOLET: Including your lap dog spying on them.

MOMMA: Yeah, well, everybody was doin' it.

Scene 13

> *On The Red Dragon. Time is a couple of weeks after the previous scene. Enter CARDINAL, disguised as a priest. ROSE is working the roulette wheel. CARDINAL watches her. MOMMA watches CARDINAL watching ROSE. JOHNNY watches MOMMA watching CARDINAL watching ROSE.*

ROSE: On the red, number six, ladies and gents… Place your bets please…

Sees CARDINAL.

Holy doodle! What are you doing here?!

CARDINAL: Can we talk, Luce?

ROSE: It's Rose! Listen, this is a private club, and there'll be hell to pay if they find you here.

MOMMA: Rosa, ya got trouble? Oh, forgive me Father.

CARDINAL: Not at all, Madam.

MOMMA: Mind me askin' how ya got in here?

CARDINAL: Father...

ROSE: O'Leary...is an old friend of my family.

CARDINAL: *(Irish accent.)* Lu...Rose's mother asked me to check up on the girl. And Rose, bless her, knows my little weakness. Between you and me, Madam, all the prayer in the world can't seem to shake my need for a wee flutter now and then. Cards. You must be the infamous, Mrs. Bigellini.

MOMMA: Call me Momma.

CARDINAL: If it's not too much to ask, Momma, might I have a moment alone with the girl?

MOMMA: I'll cover, but I've got a little gem in the oven I need to rescue in five minutes. Osso bucco. I'm salivatin' thinkin' of that marrow. Suckin' it out of the bones. Say, would ya care to join me? Got a great little Chianti pantin' in my private compartment.

CARDINAL: Ta. Sounds delightful, but I'm woefully short on time.

MOMMA: Pleasure to have a gentleman of your calibre onboard, Father O'Leary. Come back anytime. For a flutter on the tables or an intimate feed. But sign in next time.

MOMMA takes the roulette table.

Place your bets, ladies and gents.

CARDINAL: Let's go.

ROSE and CARDINAL move off. JOHNNY keeps watch.

ROSE: Shh! How did you find me?

CARDINAL: I followed my nose. This place reeks.

ROSE: How are Mummy and Daddy?

CARDINAL: They're worried sick, Bonehead. You've gained weight.

ROSE: Look, it's good to see you. Really. And I'll write them, I promise, but...

He grabs her and kisses her.

Are you nuts?!

CARDINAL: Let's get out of here while the girl I remember is still intact.

ROSE: Too late. She's gone and, honestly, I regret nothing, not one oyster.

CARDINAL: ...

ROSE: Look, meet me tomorrow, three o'clock. I'm going to the pictures: Douglas Fairbanks is starring in *The Thief of Baghdad*!

CARDINAL: Now.

Begins to drag her. JOHNNY is suddenly right there.

ROSE: Get your hands off me! Johnny?! Will you show Father O'Leary out please? I've got to get back to my table.

JOHNNY: Pleasure. Father…

    ROSE moves to roulette table and CARDINAL begins to follow.

    Don't even think about it! Nobody, and especially no priest body, messes with our girls. Capiche?

CARDINAL: You're an angry man, Son. Have you tried confiding in our Lord?

JOHNNY: Don't fuck with me. Momma's waitin'.

    Lights up on MOMMA finishing a meal. JOHNNY frisks CARDINAL.

    Clean.

MOMMA: Where's your manners, Johnny? Give the man a bowl of the special bolognese. Osso bucco's oh so gone-o.

CARDINAL: I couldn't.

    He's served a bowl.

    Thanks. I could eat a horse.

MOMMA: That's what makes it 'Special'. Jokin'!

CARDINAL: You're an artist.

    BIG MAN enters.

MOMMA: Where's your manners, Shannon? Say hello to Father O'Leary.

BIG MAN: *(Looking up.)* You! This guy's no priest.

CARDINAL: Father O'Leary, Sir.

MOMMA: Knock it off. If you're an Irish man I'm the Queen of Sheba. Johnny?

    He secures CARDINAL and begins to push his fingers back…hard.

MOMMA: Who are ya?!

CARDINAL: Aah!

BIG MAN: Hey, Momma, relax. He's a railway dick. Inspector Frank Cardinal, Canadian Pacific.

MOMMA: Well, well. Chief…what brings ya to the Dragon…really?

CARDINAL: The girl.

MOMMA: Johnny!

JOHNNY goes for his fingers again.

BIG MAN: He's tellin' the truth. Poor bastard's got a thing for Rosie.

CARDINAL: *(To BIG MAN.)* What the hell have you done to her?!

BIG MAN: Nothin' she didn't want.

CARDINAL: I will kill you!

JOHNNY: Want for me to break them this time, Momma?

MOMMA: Wait a sec. Nice work, Shannon. Now get the girl out of here. Take her for a walk, or better still…a good feed… Oysters might be nice. Hmm?

BIG MAN: I'll stay.

MOMMA: Now, Shannon.

He exits muttering.

What'ya know about my operation, Chief? Cat got your tongue?

MOMMA begins to feed him.

There's nothin' I hate more than dinner guests what don't clean their plates. Open the tunnel, here comes the train! Whoo! Whoo! What do you know about the Dragon?

He tries to speak, but she's shovelling food down his throat.

CARDINAL: Dr...dr...ugs, uh, stop, ewwhh!

(*Gagging.*), sex, ill...egal sex acts, minors.

MOMMA: What's that? I can't understand a word the poor man's saying! You take over, Johnny. Feed him up good.

JOHNNY: My pleasure.

CARDINAL: The girl for my silence.

MOMMA: Madonna! I don't do trades.

CARDINAL: One hair on her head so much as mussed, and you'll get nothing... but grief.

MOMMA: Enjoy the Bolognese, Inspector Cardinal. A railway dick from Kamloops...what's next?

She exits. Lights fade on JOHNNY feeding CARDINAL and shift to...

Scene 14

Interior of a Catholic Church. A life sized Virgin Mary is highlighted. Enter MOMMA.

MOMMA: Oh, that hurts, little Momma. Sears right down to the bone. Blessed knees are not what they used to be. I like to think you and I understand one another, so I'll cut to the marrow. There's a girl, works in my club, calls herself Rose Wood, up to somethin' no good with my son. Little slut's got my boy twisted 'round her baby finger. Oh, but Shannon's a disappointment to me these days. I've seen the way he's lookin' at me. The way he's lookin' at her. Tongue hangin' out. What do you do when you're only son's a disappointment, little Momma? Even yours, at times, eh? Let's face it, and I mean no disrespect, but our Lord Jesus got Himself into some serious scrapes. He could not have been an easy kid. So here I am askin' for help, advice, whatever you can do for me.

Virgin Mary comes to life. Is seen and heard in Her new guise only by MOMMA.

VIRGIN MARY: I'm no fortune teller, Anna.

MOMMA: Holy Mother of God!

VIRGIN MARY: In the spirit. But seriously, watch your back. If a child doesn't get the love and respect he needs at home, he goes looking for it elsewhere.

MOMMA: But...is this a joke?! Alright, who's behind this?! Come on out!

JOHNNY: Everything OK, Momma?

Virgin Mary freezes wherever she is.

MOMMA: BACK OFF!

Virgin's back to life.

VIRGIN MARY: Oh ye of little faith. You talk my ear off, and as soon as I reply and, heaven forbid, you don't like the answer...doubt.

MOMMA: No, no, never you. Me, my brain, my ears, my son...but never you little Momma.

VIRGIN MARY: Me, me, me. And, furthermore, I am not your 'little' Momma. Respect, Anna. That's the ticket.

MOMMA: Holy Mary, Mother of God, forgive me, but what...

VIRGIN MARY: That's enough for today. Think on it, and I'll see you next week.

MOMMA: Tomorrow?

VIRGIN MARY: Anna, Anna, Anna...I'm a busy woman. It just
              never stops.

MOMMA: But...

VIRGIN MARY: Next week. Ciao.

                   Virgin Mary freezes.

MOMMA: Johnny!

                   He enters running.

JOHNNY: What?!

MOMMA: Help me up. And put that pistol away now. You're
              in God's house. Where's Cardinal?

JOHNNY: The warehouse. I'm havin' a little fun before I
              finish him—

MOMMA: No! We're lettin' him go.

JOHNNY: What?!

MOMMA: I wanna know what's goin' on between him and
              that girl.

JOHNNY: What if he goes to the cops?

MOMMA: He won't. Not while we got the girl. Just don't lose
              him. And keep your eyes on that son of mine.
              Capiche?

JOHNNY: I'm your man.

MOMMA: Come here and give Momma a big kiss.

JOHNNY: Yes, Ma'am.

VIRGIN MARY: Respect, Anna.

                   *Only MOMMA hears this. She immediately pulls
                   out of the kiss, crosses herself.*

JOHNNY: What? What?!

MOMMA: We're goin' home.

JOHNNY: Ooh, I like it when Momma's in a hurry.

> *Lights shift. VIOLET speaks, MOMMA responds and JOHNNY freezes. MOMMA crosses back to join VIOLET in the hotel room. JOHNNY and VIRGIN MARY exit as focus goes to hotel.*

VIOLET: The Virgin Mary spoke to you?

MOMMA: I got a special connection, a pipeline. And now it's your Poppa. What?!

VIOLET: I'm sorry, but this is all pretty hard to swallow.

MOMMA: You think I'd make this shit up? Why would I?

VIOLET: I can't even begin to imagine.

MOMMA: You're the writer in the family. Me, I'm a simple business woman.

VIOLET: I need to sleep now.

MOMMA: Sure. Been a long day, all the way from California. I'll let myself out, eh. And I'll expect ya tomorrow.

VIOLET: And you'll finish the story.

MOMMA: Three o'clock.

VIOLET: Good night.

MOMMA: Ciao, Cara. Me and your Poppa, we're proud of ya.

> *MOMMA exits. VIOLET tosses and turns in bed. A full moon shines in through her window. Snippets of the day's stories and the sounds of trains—steaming, whistling, chug-chugging, crashing, exploding—replay in her head as she thrashes and struggles to sleep. CARDINAL, BIG MAN and CONDUCTOR are heard, but from off.*

VIOLET: *(Reading and remembering.)* I'll disappear right off that train and out of his life.

CARDINAL: Marry me!

VIOLET: First stop Vancouver. I'll take care of 'things' there and, then, after I've made some dough... Hollywood, California here I come.

CARDINAL: Marry me!

VIOLET: Frankie, just kiss me goodbye. Whoa! That is not the kind of kiss I had in mind.

CARDINAL: Marry me.

CONDUCTOR: All aboard!

BIG MAN: Close family, eh? *(Smooching noise.)*

CARDINAL: You've gained weight.

BIG MAN: A sweet, ripe, round belly.

VIOLET: *(As herself.)* What 'things' was she going to take care of?!

> *She gets up and, looking for answers, opens the suitcase. She removes ROSE's lingerie from the case and dresses in or holds the slip up against her body. She indulges, delights in the closeness to her mother, the sensual nature of the garments, her own body. She inspects herself, pirouettes, runs her hands over her body, cupping her breasts and then her own, flat belly.*

A sweet, ripe, round belly.

End of Act I.

Act II

Scene 1

> *Fifteen minutes have passed. Sound of typewriter keys in the darkness. Lights up to find VIOLET, still in her mother's lingerie, at the typewriter. CARDINAL enters in shadow. He darts to VIOLET's window and watches from the street. VIOLET finishes typing then reaches into the bag. She takes the little red belt out of the suitcase. She flicks it once, twice, three times: a lion tamer. CARDINAL reacts and his movement attracts VIOLET. As she watches in horror, he opens his mouth wide and howls like a wolf. She screams. He exits, running. VIOLET puts on a robe. CARDINAL knocks on the door.*

VIOLET: Go away!

> *Knocking continues and gets louder, more aggressive.*

I'll call the cops!

> *CARDINAL smashes the door. VIOLET screams out the window.*

Help! Somebody please! Help me!

> *CARDINAL bursts through the door. He lifts his head and howls again.*

CARDINAL: I saw you! I heard you! The two of you. You think I'll just lie down and take it. While you lie with the wolf.

VIOLET: Help me please! There's a madman in my room!

             CARDINAL grabs VIOLET around the neck and shoulders. She is choking.

CARDINAL: You like it.

VIOLET: Don't hurt me.

CARDINAL: Hurt you? Me? Ha! Me hurt you?!

VIOLET: Please.

CARDINAL: Lie down.

VIOLET: No, please.

CARDINAL: LIE DOWN.

VIOLET: Help!

CARDINAL: *(Pulling out his opium pipe.)* You need a smoke.

VIOLET: No, really.

CARDINAL: Stick this in your mouth and suck. Just like old times.

             Thanks to you, Rose Wood, I've become an expert Dragon Chaser. A dab hand.

             He smokes then passes it back to her.

VIOLET: You're confused.

CARDINAL: SMOKE!

             He forces her head down and she does.

VIOLET: I'm not Rose.

CARDINAL: Again.

             She smokes.

             See? The muscles in your neck are beginning to soften. A good sign.

VIOLET: Mmmm. I hope my head doesn't fall off.

VIOLET takes the pipe and smokes.

CARDINAL: Weaklings. The pair of us. I should have knocked you out that night and carried you home to Kamloops.

VIOLET: What night?

Shift to signify move into the past and CARDINAL's memory; he has come to ROSE after being released from imprisonment in MOMMA's warehouse. He has been hurt. ROSE has been smoking opium and he finds her lying on her bed.

CARDINAL: Luce.

ROSE: Frank? What happened to you?!

CARDINAL: Momma, Johnny.

ROSE: But why?

CARDINAL: You and your Big Man.

ROSE: You've got to get out of here. Now.

CARDINAL: I won't leave without you.

ROSE: You're bleeding.

Enter MOMMA and JOHNNY in train corridor.

MOMMA: Rosa?

ROSE: Holy Mother of God! Yes, Momma?

MOMMA: Open up. I got somethin' for ya.

ROSE: I'm just lying down.

MOMMA: Open up I said. It's not every day my son gets engaged.

CARDINAL: Engaged?!

Ready to clobber MOMMA.

CARDINAL: Let her in.

ROSE: Coming. *(To CARDINAL.)* Don't even think about it. Now hide!

MOMMA: Ya got a man in there or somethin'?

ROSE: Ha, ha! Just making myself decent, Momma.

CARDINAL sees and picks up the opium & pipe.

CARDINAL: Jesus!

ROSE: Get out of sight!

He does.

MOMMA: Johnny, you stay put.

JOHNNY: Sure thing.

JOHNNY stays in corridor. MOMMA enters and presents ROSE with the Bible.

MOMMA: The Family Bible. To welcome you into the fold.

ROSE: *(Reads dedication.)* 'To Rosa with love from M.' Thank you.

MOMMA: To be perfectly honest, I never thought anybody'd be nuts enough to take Shannon on.

ROSE: But Shannon's—

MOMMA: Yeah, yeah. That's the first time I seen my boy in Church for years. Don't think I ain't appreciative.

ROSE: Oh, well...

MOMMA: We Catholic girls gotta stick together, eh? The two of us partner up, and he might really make somethin' of himself...in the after life. It's a joke, kid! Now, how's that grandchild of mine doin'?

ROSE: Lively! I think she's going to be a dancer or a prize fighter.

MOMMA: She?

ROSE: I just know.

MOMMA: Yeah, well, I figured Shannon was gonna be a girl. Some joke, eh.

             She sinks slowly down onto her knees.

             Damn! Help me down. Bum knee.

             Head on ROSE's stomach.

             Hello Sweet Pea! Your Grand Momma's lookin' forward to meetin' ya. What's that? Ya better believe I'm gonna cook for ya. Every single day.

             She makes a smooching noise, 'kisses' baby.

             Ciao Cara. Give me a hand up, Rosa. So…we're gonna celebrate tomorrow night at dinner, eh. Oysters! Just thinkin' about them gets me hot. (*Sniffs.*) Say…you smell opium?

ROSE: What? No!

MOMMA: I'm gonna give ya credit here for the brains God gave a monkey. I'll assume ya haven't touched the stuff. That smell lingers somethin' awful, and there's others on this train been smokin' regular. But let me give ya a little word of advice, Miss Rose Wood. If I find ya been smokin' or ingestin' poison while you're carryin' my grandchild, you're gonna wish ya never been born. Capiche?

ROSE: I don't know what you're talking about.

MOMMA: Don't fuck with me! Capiche?

ROSE: Yes, Momma.

MOMMA: We'll be watchin' ya. Johnny, ya still there?

JOHNNY: You know it.

MOMMA: I'm gonna have a lie down. Wake me in a couple of hours.

JOHNNY: I'm countin' the minutes.

MOMMA: He's my gooood boy.

She exits. CARDINAL reappears.

CARDINAL: You stupid little bitch!

ROSE: Ow!

CARDINAL: When's the baby due? When?!

ROSE: May.

CARDINAL: No. You were—

ROSE: Oh! She's kicking! Feel.

CARDINAL: No more drugs. Do you hear me?!

ROSE: You're not my father.

CARDINAL: But I'm hers.

ROSE: No.

CARDINAL: I don't believe you.

ROSE: And I'm engaged.

CARDINAL: Shannon Bigellini's a two-bit drug dealer. And what about your precious dreams?!

ROSE: We're going to California.

CARDINAL: Not with him. Jesus! Not with him!

He grabs ROSE's bag violently and rips the lining.

ROSE: Look what you've done! You've ripped it! My bag from Mummy.

CARDINAL: You care more about that God damned bag than me.

ROSE: Frankie, you and me, we were just… experimenting.

CARDINAL: No.

ROSE: I'm in love with Shannon.

CARDINAL: I'm lost.

ROSE: You will be if we don't get you away from here. Lock the door, get into my bed, and keep your face covered.

CARDINAL: But…?

ROSE: Just lie still.

She prepares to leave. Buckles the little red belt around her waist.

Try to sleep. I'm going for help.

Scene 2

JOHNNY's room. He's lifting weights. Knock on the door.

JOHNNY: Yeah?

ROSE: It's me.

JOHNNY: This is a surprise. What can I do for ya, Tasty?

ROSE: I need your help.

JOHNNY: Again?

ROSE: My friend, he's in trouble.

JOHNNY: Father O'Leary?

ROSE: Very funny. He's here.

JOHNNY: Dumb shit.

ROSE: Johnny, I need to get him away. To a doctor. He's
             been hurt.

JOHNNY: Tell me one reason I shouldn't just turn him over to
             Momma.

ROSE: He's like my brother.

JOHNNY: So?

ROSE: He's a good man.

JOHNNY: Yawn.

ROSE: Same deal as last time.

JOHNNY: Hey, hey, hey! It's my lucky day.

ROSE: You promise to help him?

JOHNNY: Your wish is my command. Come here.

ROSE: Momma's just around the corner!

JOHNNY: The old girl took a pill. She'll sleep like a grizzly
             bear for another couple of hours. Mmm, you feel
             mighty fine. Give it to me!

                    ROSE unbuckles the little belt.

ROSE: Hands off. I give the orders now. Get down on your
             belly and crawl, Worm.

                    *He does and howls like a wolf. She brings the belt
                    down on his backside and he whimpers. This is hard
                    for ROSE. She is probably in tears.*

             Every time you howl, I hit. Understood?

                    He howls and she hits.

             Bad boy. Drop your drawers and bend over.

                    JOHNNY howls and ROSE hits. Shift back to 1949

and the distraught CARDINAL who has, in fact, been telling this story. He makes tiny howling noises, more like whimpers. VIOLET considers the wreck of a man.

VIOLET: Sleep now, Mr. Cardinal.

VIOLET examines the red bag once again for clues: runs her hands over it, empties it completely, shakes it, again, and again, and harder. Something's in there. She finds a rip which has been carefully repaired—sewn by MOMMA—and tears it open again. She finds the other diary.

(*Reading.*) I wanted it all, and then I took it, everything I could get my hands on. And I ran, but I didn't count on the child. Or the father.

Scene 3

We move into ROSE's diary and a fog filled night on Skid Row. Suspicious and unhealthy looking people loom out of the fog. ROSE enters carrying a slip of paper with an address on it.

DRUGGIE: Hey, girlie.

ROSE: Oh!

DRUGGIE: You selling?

ROSE: No!

DRUGGIE: Buying? I can take you to a good place. For a couple of bucks you can get some quality smoke, put your head down for a while.

ROSE: Leave me alone!

MOTHER
CUTTER: You heard the lady. Piss off.

DRUGGIE: Piss you, asshole.

CUTTER: Clever, very clever.

DRUGGIE: I piss on you.

CUTTER: Clear away, you dribbling fart.

DRUGGIE: I've got a perfect right to occupy this space.

CUTTER: Grrrrrrr!

DRUGGIE: Caw! Caw!

CUTTER: *(Calling.)* Constable Cullen! Sir, we've got a problem! Shithead here's molesting another young lady.

DRUGGIE: Fuck!

      Exits.

CUTTER: Asshole. *(To ROSE.)* A most vivid figment of my imagination: the jolly old Constable. Abigail Cutter at your service.

ROSE: You're Mother Cutter?

CUTTER: Who's asking?

ROSE: A friend said you might be able to help me.

CUTTER: So you're carrying a little extra baggage?

ROSE: Yes.

CUTTER: Who sent you?

ROSE: Johnny Jones.

CUTTER: You'll have to do better than that, Dearie.

ROSE: He said to remind you of the big girl from Gimli.

CUTTER: Ha! That Johnny Jones. You're not his usual type.

ROSE: It's not like that.

CUTTER: If you say so. Come on in. We can't talk business out here. Drink?

ROSE: It's a little early for me.

CUTTER: Let's get this straight. There's risks. No guarantees.

ROSE: I know.

CUTTER: For the record, I'm good at what I do. Lots of practice. The human race hasn't improved over the years; just multiplied. What do you think of my operating room?

ROSE: This?

CUTTER: You bring pads, Biscuit?

ROSE: Pads?

CUTTER: For the blood. Takes no time at all. How far along are you?

ROSE: Thirteen weeks. I think.

CUTTER: Fifty bucks.

ROSE: But...this is going to wipe me out.

CUTTER: Close the door behind you on the way out.

ROSE: When?!

CUTTER: What's say we plunge right in, Dumpling?

Shift. MOTHER CUTTER freezes.

ROSE: She pins me down; straps me to a kitchen table. Gotcha! I rise, a white bird hovering over the scene of the crime. Crumbs, I swear, dear Lord, there are crumbs on the oilcloth under my buttocks. And she rips the girl's panties off and hoists her skirt up to her shoulders. I can't breath. And down the rabbit hole it slides. Cold, ripping, and...and blood...

everywhere. Frank's child drowning in the crumbs on a kitchen table.

CARDINAL: NO!

Shift out of the diary. CARDINAL clings to VIOLET and buries his head in her lap. She allows this briefly then gently pushes him away.

VIOLET: Mr. Cardinal. Shh. Shh.

CARDINAL prepares a pipe. He smokes and passes it to VIOLET.

CARDINAL: Close the book.

She smokes.

Do you still love trains? Luce?

VIOLET: Violet.

He produces the little train.

CARDINAL: I bought this for you. It was in the bag that brought you back to me. Give me your hand.

VIOLET: Inspector Cardinal...

CARDINAL: Frank. Frankie.

He gently places the train in the palm of her hand.

CARDINAL: Close your eyes, Sweetheart.

VIOLET: Who am I?

CARDINAL: Close them. We're going home.

VIOLET: We are?

He lies beside her or pulls her back to lean against him then slowly, sensuously runs the train up one arm and then down the other arm.

CARDINAL: Can you see the train tracks stretching out in front of you?

VIOLET: No... Yes!

CARDINAL: Can you hear the crickets? Feel the hot, dry grass tickling your bare ankles? The warm breeze blowing through your hair? There's a strand in your eye.

VIOLET: It stings.

CARDINAL: I'll brush it away.

VIOLET: That's better.

Train whistle in the distance.

CARDINAL: Listen! It's coming. Can you feel it coming?

VIOLET: Oh God. I can.

CARDINAL: Through the soles of your feet.

VIOLET: Don't stop. Please.

CARDINAL: My turn.

He gives her the train. She runs the train over his body.

VIOLET: Like this?

CARDINAL: Slowly.

He presses her head to his heart.

CARDINAL: Listen. Can you hear it?

VIOLET: It's coming.

They embrace. Shift and we move into the 20s.

Scene 5

> *ROSE's diary. She sings 'California, Here I Come...' to Baby Violet. CARDINAL is with them. He returns ROSE's crucifix.*

CARDINAL: I have something for Violet, too.

ROSE: A tiny train! Violet, you've got an admirer. Whoo! Whoo!

> *She runs the tiny train over Violet's tiny body and down the underside of CARDINAL's wrist.*

CARDINAL: Come home, Luce. Let me look after you both.

ROSE: Oh, Frankie! I've been so lonely. Momma keeps Biggie running or glued to her side. I'm beginning to think we're never going to make it to California.

CARDINAL: Jesus Christ!

ROSE: What?

CARDINAL: Have you looked in the mirror lately, Miss Gish? You're a wreck.

ROSE: I'm tired. You think it's easy being a mother?

> *CARDINAL is searching for the drugs.*

ROSE: What are you doing?

CARDINAL: Drug addicts make lousy actresses. And foul mothers.

ROSE: You're jealous! You've always been jealous!

> *He finds the pipe and the lacquer box with opium.*

ROSE: Give me that!

CARDINAL: You listen to me. We're taking Violet and getting the hell out of here. You're gonna clean up.

ROSE: I'm not leaving. Not without Biggie.

CARDINAL: Christ!

ROSE: Where are you going?!

CARDINAL: You smash everything!

ROSE: No! Please, don't leave me!

She clings to him. BIG MAN enters.

BIG MAN: Get your fuckin' hands off my wife!

ROSE: It's not what you think!

CARDINAL: Have you even looked at her lately? Her eyes? Her skin? You like this?

ROSE: Stop it!

CARDINAL: Maybe you get your kisses somewhere else now, eh.

ROSE: No!

BIG MAN: Come on, little man!

CARDINAL: My pleasure.

ROSE: Stop it! Both of you!

They begin to fight.

(To VIOLET.) My Baby! Mommy's here. *(To CARDINAL and BIG MAN.)* Stop it!

Enter MOMMA and JOHNNY. JOHNNY fires a pistol and hits CARDINAL in the leg.

BIG MAN: Fuck!

ROSE: Frank!

MOMMA: Get up! Both of ya! Johnny, take that son of a bitch into my 'office' and beat the crap out of him. Then we'll have a serious talk.

CARDINAL: Let's talk now.

> *MOMMA signals and JOHNNY hurts CARDINAL.*

ROSE: /No!

BIG MAN: /I was dealin' with this.

MOMMA: Button it!

BIG MAN: Jesus, Momma! RESPECT!

> *MOMMA's winding up to smack him, but stops when he says 'respect'.*

MOMMA: Rose, give me Violet.

ROSE: I'd rather die!

> *MOMMA goes for ROSE.*

BIG MAN: Nobody touches my wife!

JOHNNY: That's not what I heard.

> *BIG MAN lunges at JOHNNY.*

MOMMA: BACK OFF! What's the hell's got into everybody?!

JOHNNY: Sorry, Momma.

BIG MAN: Give Violet to me, Rose.

ROSE: But...

BIG MAN: Now!

MOMMA: Get his ass out of here!

JOHNNY: After you, 'Father'.

> *JOHNNY pushes CARDINAL and ROSE attacks JOHNNY with the crucifix, digging at his face. In the scuffle, CARDINAL breaks free and ROSE and JOHNNY fall to the ground. ROSE hangs on to JOHNNY.*

ROSE: Run Frank!

JOHNNY: /Aaah!

CARDINAL: /Lucy!

JOHNNY: /Bitch!

BIG MAN: /Rosie!

MOMMA: /Johnny!

ROSE: Go, Frank! Run!

               FRANK hobbles free.

MOMMA: What the hell are ya waiting' for?!

               MOMMA exits. JOHNNY peels ROSE off with a struggle, then exits, running. ROSE holds the broken crucifix. BIG MAN holds Baby Violet.

ROSE: *(About the crucifix.)* He's lost two toes.

               MOMMA enters and listens.

BIG MAN: You ballin' the railway dick?!

ROSE: …

BIG MAN: Yes or no?!

ROSE: No!

MOMMA: Give me my granddaughter.

               He waves her off.

BIG MAN: Our daughter needs a proper mother. *(To VIOLET.)* Ya even know what that is? I want out.

ROSE: What?!

               He moves to ROSE.

BIG MAN: Me, Rose, and Violet are leavin' this city, Momma.

MOMMA: In a pig's eye.

BIG MAN: I want my cut. What's due to me.

MOMMA: No.

BIG MAN: No? No?! ·

MOMMA: You'd die on your own.

BIG MAN: We're dyin' here. Do ya even care?

MOMMA: Ya can't even take care of your own damned family. Look at Rosa. Look at her!

BIG MAN: … Rosie?

MOMMA: Who's feedin' it to her? You? Where's she get it?

BIG MAN: I don't know. Skid Row?

MOMMA: Bullshit. She's stealin' from the Dragon.

ROSE: No!

MOMMA: Someone is. And that's your cut down the toilet, Mister. Or should I say 'up in smoke'?

BIG MAN: Rosie? You stealin' from us?

ROSE: No.

MOMMA: Ha!

BIG MAN: Don't lie to me!

ROSE: I wouldn't! I didn't!

BIG MAN: Where then?! Where do ya get it?! I'll shake the truth out of ya!

ROSE: Stop it! This isn't you!

MOMMA: Ya sure about that?

ROSE: Johnny. I get it from Johnny Jones.

BIG MAN: What?!

MOMMA: Pathetic.

She grabs VIOLET.

ROSE: Violet!

MOMMA: Ya want this little girl back? Then clean up your nest, Lovebirds.

BIG MAN: Momma!

MOMMA: Come on, Sweet Pea. Grand Momma's gonna get ya a nice, warm bottle. And change that diaper.

ROSE: Violet!

MOMMA: Ya just lost your visitin' rights, Addict.

BIG MAN moves to the door to block MOMMA's exit.

BIG MAN: Momma!

MOMMA: Shannon.

BIG MAN: You cross this line and—

MOMMA: Oh my. Are Big Man and his lovely bride gonna cut the apron strings and strike out on their own? Ha! That'll be the day.

BIG MAN lunges at his mother. She pulls a pistol.

I'll use it! The two of ya ain't fit to be parents. Now pull yourself together and behave like a man. I expect your ass on the Red Dragon tonight, Mr. Big. You'll be workin' lots of extra hours to pay off Rosa's debts. Johnny'll be back for ya. The Dragon's rollin' out at 8:30. Sharp.

MOMMA exits.

ROSE: Violet! Violet!

BIG MAN: Maybe the old bitch's right.

ROSE: What?!

BIG MAN: Nice story shapin' up, eh. Drug addict and small time hood raise baby girl. Real fairy tale.

ROSE: It's over. No more drugs.

BIG MAN: That's what my Daddy used to say. Right up to the day he overdosed in Mr. Hong's fine establishment.

ROSE: I swear.

BIG MAN: Was it good?

ROSE: What?

BIG MAN: Johnny Jones don't do favours unless there's somethin' in it for him. So I repeat…was it good?!

ROSE: No!

BIG MAN: But ya just kept goin' back for more.

ROSE: He made me.

BIG MAN: Did ya do it with Violet in the room?

He howls: a tiny, eerie howl.

ROSE: Stop it!

BIG MAN: Do me, Rose. Like ya done the wolf man.

Howls again, it builds.

Hard! Here! *(His butt.)* What's the matter? Don't ya like it with your husband?

ROSE: No!

BIG MAN: No?! Oh, I'm sorry. Am I doin' somethin' wrong? Is my technique off?

ROSE: You're scaring me.

BIG MAN: How 'bout we try it like this then?!

               He moves in as if to kiss her then begins to choke her.
               She struggles briefly then goes completely limp. He
               stops.

               Rosie?! Baby?!

ROSE: We're gonna be alright. I promise.

BIG MAN: We gotta get out of this place.

ROSE: We will. We just—

               Knock on the door.

JOHNNY: You two decent?

ROSE: What's he doing here?!

JOHNNY: Ready or not, I'm comin' in.

BIG MAN: *(To ROSE.)* You, me, and Violet, we're leavin'
               tonight.

               BIG MAN hides. JOHNNY enters holding his hand
               to the cut over his eye. Big Man grabs his gun.

JOHNNY: Hey!

BIG MAN: Mr. Jones. It seems you've been a bad, busy little
               wolf while Momma and me had our backs turned.

JOHNNY: Momma knows I'm—

BIG MAN: Nasty cut. Rosie play too hard for ya this time, Mr.
               Wolf? I'd sure hate to have to tell Momma about all
               those other times.

JOHNNY: I don't know what you're—

BIG MAN: Listen up! It's time for the three of us to deal.

Scene 6

> *1949. A happy MOMMA is singing Puccini and preparing a meal. BIG MAN appears as before: a 'ghost'.*

MOMMA: I'm makin' her favourite, Shannon! Spaghetti with the big, spicy meatballs and, for the main course, osso bucco! Mmmmmm! Osso-good-o! We're gonna have some party, Baby. Just the three of us.

Scene 7

> *Moments later in 1949. Lights up to reveal JOHNNY lifting weights. Enter VIOLET.*

JOHNNY: Well, well, well. Little Flower.

VIOLET: I need your help.

JOHNNY: Good enough to pluck.

VIOLET: You were always there. Always hovering in the background, watching and listening.

JOHNNY: So?

VIOLET: So you know what happened that night on the Dragon.

JOHNNY: Bravo.

VIOLET: Were you planning to tell me?

> *He moves to her.*

You lay one finger on me and Grand Momma will know everything.

JOHNNY: Have a heart, Flower.

VIOLET: Like you and my mother. This is some cushy life you've got here.

JOHNNY: She knows.

VIOLET: Not a chance.

JOHNNY: There ain't nothin' that woman don't know. Cept' what's in your head. And maybe, just maybe, where that suitcase of your mother's came from out of the blue.

VIOLET: What's that supposed to mean?

JOHNNY: Means I sent it.

VIOLET: You?! How the hell...?

JOHNNY: Bet ya learned a whole lot about Rosa last night from 'Uncle Frank'.

VIOLET: You've been spying on me since I stepped off that train!

JOHNNY: I cannot tell a lie.

VIOLET: Swell. She pulls the strings and we all dance.

JOHNNY: Momma made big changes after the Dragon went down. On account of you.

VIOLET: What changes?

JOHNNY: Ask her.

VIOLET: Prostitution?! Narcotics?! How many lives has she destroyed?

JOHNNY: Not yours.

VIOLET: Tell me about your deal with Poppa and my Mother. The night of the accident.

JOHNNY: Just find a way to stop the train, Shannon says. As close as possible to the U.S. border. We'll take care of the rest, Rosa says.

VIOLET: What 'rest'?

JOHNNY:	They wanted what Momma owed him. His 'cut'. That's all. And then they promised they'd disappear.
VIOLET:	And?
JOHNNY:	And somethin' went awful wrong.
VIOLET:	What? Where was I that night?
JOHNNY:	Momma's been cookin' all day like a crazy woman. For you.

VIOLET exits.

Tasty.

Scene 8

Back to MOMMA. She is at the tomb again with an offering: lunch. Enter VIOLET. She watches.

MOMMA:	Our Little Girl stood us up, Shannon. Shannon?
VIOLET:	Grand Momma.
MOMMA:	Violet! Have ya eaten, Baby?
VIOLET:	No.
MOMMA:	Here. Your Poppa won't mind. Between you and me, his appetite these days is lousy.
VIOLET:	We need to talk.
MOMMA:	As soon as I see ya take a mouthful of this-
VIOLET:	I found Mother's red diary.
MOMMA:	...
VIOLET:	There are pages missing. They were cut out. Recently.

You lied to me.

MOMMA:	…
VIOLET:	Crossed my heart and lied! Why?!
MOMMA:	Little girl—
VIOLET:	No!
MOMMA:	I couldn't stand to see ya hurt.
VIOLET:	My father's dead. My mother disappeared. He was running drugs. She was a drug addict. A prostitute. And my Grandmother made it all possible.
MOMMA:	Baby…
VIOLET:	Dish it out or lose me.

> *MOMMA presents VIOLET with the missing diary pages.*

MOMMA:	She didn't want you, Violet.

> *Shift and we are in the diary.*

Scene 9

> *ROSE's compartment. JOHNNY is in the corridor, lurking. ROSE kneels and begins to pray. BIG MAN enters with a small case and surprises her.*

ROSE:	Hail Mary full of Grace, the Lord is with Thee. Blessed…
BIG MAN:	'The time has come, the walrus said…'.
ROSE:	Crazy man.
BIG MAN:	Hey, are those tears? Did somebody do somethin' to hurt ya? Momma? Johnny? I'll kill that bastard.
ROSE:	No!

BIG MAN: What then?

ROSE: I did something awful.

BIG MAN: Nah. Not you, Rosie.

ROSE: Yes, me. And now the whole damned nightmare's beginning again.

BIG MAN: What nightmare?

ROSE: I was pregnant when I met you.

BIG MAN: No! I don't wanna hear—

ROSE: The baby was Frank's.

BIG MAN: You love him?!

ROSE: I had it seen to. There's this woman on Skid Row. They call her Cutter and—

BIG MAN: Aw, Rosie, no.

ROSE: I've been stupid, stupid, stupid! Well, no more. I'm leaving.

BIG MAN: You love the Cardinal?!

ROSE: No! Not like that. Biggie—

BIG MAN: Look what I got.

            He takes a table cloth from his case and spreads it out.

            Italian bread, wine, asiago cheese, and pears. Ripe. Soft and sweet. We're having a picnic. And you can tell your Big Man everything. You think this happens every day? What we got?

ROSE: No.

BIG MAN: I fell like a ton of bricks on that train from Kamloops.

ROSE: Me, too.

BIG MAN: Marry me, Rosie.

ROSE: I'm going to California if it kills me.

BIG MAN: Do you love me? Do you love me, Miss Rose
               Wood?!

ROSE: I do.

BIG MAN: Ha! She loves me! We'll go together.

ROSE: She'll never let you go.

BIG MAN: I'll open a restaurant. 'Food To Die For'. And you'll
               be the next Miss Lillian Gish.

ROSE: I'm pregnant! Again. It's yours.

BIG MAN: Jesus, Mary, and Uncle Joseph. I'm gonna be a
               daddy?

ROSE: Yes… unless…

BIG MAN: Unless?

ROSE: You see, I really don't think I should have it. I think
               you and me should start fresh, honest.

BIG MAN: We're Catholics for Christ's sake.

ROSE: What happened to lapsed?

BIG MAN: Rosie, Baby, I'm gonna be the best God damned
               daddy the world has ever known. Not like my old
               man. So? I'm on my knees here.

ROSE: We're getting married? And going to California?

BIG MAN: We're having a baby! Man oh man! Let's celebrate.
               I've got just the thing. Prepare to chase the dragon,
               little lady.

ROSE: Opium?

BIG MAN: *(Tempting.)* An experience.

ROSE: I've seen some of the people in here, and in *Broken Blossoms,* that poor man, he was ruined.

BIG MAN: Losers, Hollywood. I'm talkin' 'once'.

ROSE: But what if I like it too much?

BIG MAN: You gonna buy the stuff? Not from me you're not, 'Mommy'.

ROSE: So you do sell drugs.

BIG MAN: I'm an errand boy. But not for long. Off with her head!

                JOHNNY enters.

JOHNNY: Excuse me Rosa, Shannon. Wrong compartment.

BIG MAN: Johnny. This will be our, uh, little secret, eh. Momma doesn't need to know. Got it?

JOHNNY: Hear no evil, see no evil, smell no evil.

                Takes money offered by BIG MAN and exits.

ROSE: I don't like that man.

BIG MAN: *(Comforting.)* Here, lean back against me. I'll hold the pipe. Nice, eh?

ROSE: Nice.

                They smoke and get very comfortable. Shift into…

Scene 10

The night of the train wreck. Train wreck as played out at the beginning of the play. Following the crash, ROSE emerges from the wreck.

ROSE: Biggie! Biggie?!

She discovers him in the rubble.

Holy Mary Mother of God! I'm coming, Biggie, I'm coming!

She tries to get him out. JOHNNY emerges from the wreck.

Johnny! Help me!

JOHNNY: Christ. Move over.

JOHNNY touches BIG MAN and steps back immediately.

ROSE: No!

JOHNNY: Rosa, stop.

She keeps working.

JOHNNY: He's dead.

ROSE: No! No! No!

MOMMA: *(From the wreckage upstage.)* Shannon!

JOHNNY: Thank Christ! Over here, Momma.

ROSE stops his mouth.

ROSE: Shhh! I'm gonna need a full five minutes.

JOHNNY: What the hell are ya talkin' about?

ROSE rifles through BIG MAN's pockets and finds a number of bills: his 'cut'.

MOMMA: *(Getting closer.)* Shannon! Where are ya, Baby?!

ROSE: We still have a deal, Mr. Jones. Don't let me down.

> *JOHNNY watches as ROSE walks into the night.
> MOMMA appears in time to see her disappear.
> Shift as VIOLET breaks out of the scene and speaks
> directly to MOMMA.*

VIOLET: Bullshit!

MOMMA: Violet! I saw her. I saw Rosa leave that night.

VIOLET: Poppa and my Mother had a plan. She would
           never, ever have walked away without me. I know
           that now. But I'll walk away from you. Like that.
           One more lie and I'm gone.

MOMMA: Violet—

VIOLET: I can do it.

> *VIOLET moves back to JOHNNY to take ROSE's
> place. MOMMA deliberates and we shift back to the
> story.*

MOMMA: *(Getting closer.)* Shannon! Where are ya, Baby?!

ROSE: We still have a deal, Mr. Jones. Now tell me where
           Violet is. Quick!

JOHNNY: I thought the kid was with you.

ROSE: You lying bastard! WHERE IS SHE?!

> *Enter MOMMA as ROSE launches an attack on
> JOHNNY.*

ROSE: Where's my baby?! /We had a deal!

MOMMA: /Enough! Hold onto her, Johnny. Good boy. I
           thought I lost ya.

JOHNNY: Not a chance.

MOMMA: Where's Shannon?

JOHNNY: …

MOMMA: Johnny?!

ROSE: He's dead!

MOMMA: …

ROSE: We were running away from you. He's dead because of you!

JOHNNY: Shut your hole!

> *MOMMA keens.*

JOHNNY: Momma?!

> *She keens.*

JOHNNY: Jesus, look what ya done!

ROSE: I want my Baby. Give me my Baby!

MOMMA: Violet…

ROSE: What?

MOMMA: She was with me.

ROSE: No.

MOMMA: Violet's gone. /They're both gone.

ROSE: /No! No. No. No. No. No. Take me to her!

MOMMA: Ya don't want that.

ROSE: Now!

MOMMA: She's bad. Her face…

ROSE: Violet.

MOMMA: That's right. Cry. Let it out. Let it all out.

MOMMA reaches out to comfort ROSE.

ROSE: Keep your hands off me!

*ROSE exits. JOHNNY and MOMMA watch her
go. The sound of a baby crying is heard: VIOLET.
JOHNNY, surprised, turns to MOMMA who
gestures he is to keep his mouth shut. He moves
away from her and into the shadow of the wreckage.
Shift and VIOLET enters.*

VIOLET: Monster.

MOMMA: Baby, no. I was in shock. You gotta /understand, I

VIOLET: /How much did you pay to get rid of her?

MOMMA: She took Shannon's cut. That's all.

VIOLET: She thinks I'm dead!

MOMMA: Violet, I did it for you.

VIOLET: Three strikes. You're out!-

MOMMA: I'm a monster?! Rosa was a junkie! She probably
             died years ago in an alley with a needle in her arm!
             You met any junkies, Missy? At university? On
             your European tours? In the pictures maybe. Or
             those books you're always readin'. Well, take it
             from me, junkies don't change. And they ain't
             romantic. Nothin', nobody can compete. Not your
             Daddy. Not you. Not even God.

VIOLET: You outta know.

MOMMA: You bet. I was married to one.

VIOLET: You fed on them!

MOMMA: Look at those lily white arms of yours.

VIOLET: Ow!

MOMMA: Not a bruise. Those rosy cheeks. And those eyes.
                Clear as a baby's. I'm some monster inflictin' my
                love and money on you.

                VIOLET cries.

                Shush now, Sweet Pea. We're gonna be alright.

Scene 11

*VIOLET's hotel room. In the darkness, VIOLET
quietly sings or hums 'California, Here I Come'.
Lights up. She places ROSE's diary into the red
suitcase then closes it. She checks the room to see
that everything is packed. The toy train remains
out. She picks it up and as she does so CARDINAL
and MOMMA are dimly highlighted in isolated
areas of the wreckage. Behind them in deeper
shadow are BIG MAN (still lying where he fell in
the crash) and JOHNNY. They are all images
'conjured up in VIOLET's mind'. CARDINAL
stands with his arms outstretched, as if waiting
with LUCY for the oncoming train. MOMMA is on
her knees, praying and waiting. VIOLET studies
them then runs the little train tenderly over the
palm of her hand and the underside of her wrist. As
she does so MOMMA and CARDINAL respond:
CARDINAL shivers deliciously and MOMMA
sobs. In a decisive move, VIOLET places the toy
train in her pocket. Immediately, lights fade on
CARDINAL and MOMMA. VIOLET watches
them disappear, then picks up the red suitcase and
exits.*

The End.